AMY WYANT

MEMORY IMPROVEMENT

The Ultimate Guide on How to Sharpen Your Memory, Discover the Effective Ways to Improve Your Memory to Remember Anything

Descrierea CIP a Bibliotecii Naționale a României
AMY WYANT
    MEMORY IMPROVEMENT. The Ultimate Guide on How to Sharpen Your Memory, Discover the Effective Ways to Improve Your Memory to Remember Anything / Amy Wyant – Bucharest: Editura My Ebook, 2021
    ISBN

AMY WYANT

MEMORY IMPROVEMENT

The Ultimate Guide on How to Sharpen Your Memory, Discover the Effective Ways to Improve Your Memory to Remember Anything

My Ebook Publishing House
Bucharest, 2021

TABLE OF CONTENTS

INTRODUCTION

A good memory is truly important for anyone to possess. Your memory of faces, names, facts, information, dates, events, circumstances and other things concerning your everyday life is the measure of your ability to prevail in today's fast-paced, information-dependent society. With a good memory, you don't have to fear forgetting/misplacing important stuffs and you can overcome mental barriers that hinder you from achieving success in your career, love life, and personal life.

Your memory is composed of complicated neural connections in your brain which are believed to be capable of holding millions of data. The ability of your mind to retain past experiences in a highly organized manner gives you the potential to learn and create different ideas. Your experiences are the stepping stones to greater accomplishments and at the same time your guides and protectors from danger. If your memory serves you well in this respect, you are saved the agony of repeating the mistakes of the past. By remembering crucial lessons and circumstances, you avoid the mistakes and failures made by other people.

Unless you have an illness or handicap, a poor memory is often attributed to lack of attention or concentration, insufficient listening skills, and other inherent bad habits; however, it can be honed and developed using the right methods.

Many people believe that their memory gets worse as they get older. This is true only for those who do not use their memory properly. Memory is like a muscle - the more it is used, the better it gets. The more it is neglected, the worse it gets. This is the reason why older people have more trouble remembering than younger ones. However, people increasing in age can overcome this dilemma and can even further improve their memory by continuing their education, by refining their minds, by keeping themselves open to new experiences, and by keeping their imagination working. An important thing to realize is that different people have various ways of learning. The way in which people learn is often a factor determining the subjects they choose to study, instructors they relate to, and careers they select.

Memorization or retention of data operates by loading images, sounds, taste, smell, and sensation (touch) in a very organized and meaningful combination in our brain. There are three types of memory.

Sensory Memory is where temporary information is briefly recorded. Images such as a picture in a magazine and the design on your customer's clothing are momentarily stored in the sensory memory. It will be quickly replaced by another sensory memory unless you do something to retain it.

Short-term Memory, characterized by 20 to 30 seconds of retention, involves a limited amount of information, and is necessary in traditional processing of experiences and ordinary data gathering (everyday sensation and perception). For example, you were taught by your professor some great techniques on how to easily solve complicated Math problems. The next time you take a Math exam, you may possibly remember some of the formulas, but it's doubtful you'll be able to recall and apply all the methods being taught.

Long-term Memory involves consolidation and organization of complex knowledge and information for further reference and other cognitive (mental) processing such as the application of learning or information into meaningful experiences. Examples would include your birthday, your father's name, and your home's appearance.

Short-term and **long-term memories** are concerned with how you continually organize data that are stored in your brain. In short, human memory is like a vast and complicated yet organized library, rather than a trash can or disordered store room.

In order for you to further develop your memory capacity in various tasks, it would be helpful if you consider points and ideas in improving your memory. This would make your retention practices more efficient and sharper.

Chapter One

SHARP MEMORY FACTORS

If someone was to read a list of words to you, it's most unlikely that you will remember all the words in the list. You'll be able to recall most of the words at the beginning, some at the middle, and a few at the end. These effects are known as primacy (words at the beginning) and recency (words at the end).

The only way that a normal person can effectively recall all of the words in the list, is if he applies a mnemonic technique to help him remember. You'll also find that it's easier to recall a word if it's repeated several times in the list, or if it's related to the other words in any way, or if it stands out among the other words (for example, the word "ruby" will stand out from a list of vegetables).

To take advantage of your primacy and recency, you must find a middle ground. If you are doing something that requires a lot of thinking and you do this non-stop for hours, you'll find that the dip in the recall between the primacy and recency can be quite considerable.

If, on the other hand, you stop to take breaks too often, your brain will not really reach its primacy because it keeps on getting interrupted. In a more practical application, instead of continuously studying or working for hours, you might want to try pausing and resting after 30-50 minutes of working, just to give your brain time to refresh itself and to maximize the time when your primacy and recency are balanced.

Contrary to popular belief, being smart is not synonymous to having a good memory or good retention. You don't have to force yourself to study and understand more in order to improve your memory; the key is actually in your lifestyle, your attitude, your diet, and your habits.

You Are What You Eat

It is often said that your brain is probably the greediest organ in your body, and it requires a very specific type of nutrition from your diet. It shouldn't be surprising then that your diet affects how your brain performs, and it performs well with a steady supply of glucose. Before you go out of your house in the morning, it would be great if you can give your brain the fuel it needs by eating a hearty breakfast. A salad packed full of antioxidants, including beta-carotene and vitamins C and E, should also help keep your brain in tip-top condition by helping to reduce damaging free radicals (damaging molecules). As you grow older, your brain has lesser capacity to defend itself from daily threats like free radicals, inflammation, and oxidation. That's why aging people need more nutrition than younger ones.

Free radicals are like cavities to your teeth; they slowly build up if they're not cleaned out. As the brain cells grow older, they sometimes stop communicating with each other. As an effect, it slows down essential processes like thinking, short-term memory retrieval, and regenerating new cells. Therefore, anti-oxidants are essential to maintain not only good health, but a good memory as well. Good sources of anti-oxidants are:

- *Vitamin A and beta-carotene:* Carrots, spinach, cantaloupe, winter squash

- *Vitamin C:* Citrus fruits, broccoli, strawberries, tomatoes

- *Vitamin E:* Nuts, seeds, vegetable oil, wheat germ

Studies show that fatty food that causes artheosclerosis (clogging of arteries) are also the same type of food that disrupts neural activities. Cut back on the fat and replace it with foods rich in anti-oxidants. Nothing will replace a well-balanced meal, but to make sure that your body doesn't lack any of its nutritional needs, it would be a good idea to take food supplements. As the name implies, they're supplements, and not replacements.

Scientific research also indicates that eating fish can indeed sharpen your memory. Most fish fat contains the polyunsaturated fatty acid DHA, which performs a significant part in the brain development of young children. Tests show that kids who consume adequate foods containing DHA score better on IQ tests than those who take lesser amounts of DHA. Fish also contains omega-3 fatty acids which opens up new communication centers in the brain's neurons. This allows your mind to operate at its peak performance.

Another significant finding suggests that smoking can affect the ability of the brain to process information properly. Chain smokers have higher risks of impairing their visual and verbal memories. So the next time you think of smoking, remember that it's not only dangerous to your health, but you are sacrificing your memory functions as well.

Caffeine and alcohol causes anxiety and nervousness. This may hamper information from properly entering your mind because memory works best when you are relaxed and focused.

Reduce Stress

Medical researches show that people who are always anxious produce "stress hormones" like cortisol, which damages brain cells. Make it a point to do something that will relax you everyday. Try meditating, yoga, drinking tea, taking a long bath … whatever works for you. A very effective method to reduce stress is deep breathing and visualizing the expected outcome of any situation to turn out well. Don't forget to get enough rest.

Poor memory is often a result of poor self-image. After all, it all starts and ends in the mind. So to have a healthy mind, believe that you can achieve anything you desire. Boost your self-esteem and be confident in your abilities. Your attitude should be supportive of your goals.

Cardiovascular exercises like walking improves blood circulation and are good for the heart and brain. Research also indicates that walking helps release hormones that aid in regenerating new brain cells. If you're bored with just plain walking, engage into sports that you love. Play basketball, volleyball, tennis, or anything that excites you. By exercising, you can lessen your chances of developing high blood pressure which contributes to memory loss when you get older. So get up and get moving. Not only will you be getting a fit and healthy body, but you'll also sharpen your memory and improve your creativity. Not to mention the fun and camaraderie you'll be getting with your teammates and competitors.

Just like any muscle, you also need to exercise your brain so that it doesn't deteriorate. Engage in games that will help you think. Talk to people, read informational books, listen to educational tapes, and make it a habit to continuously learn and experience new things. Remember that when your neurons die, they don't come back to life anymore. So you better use them, or you'll lose them.

If you feel that your memory really isn't how it used to be, go and see a physician. Sometimes, memory loss can be a symptom of more serious diseases and can go undetected for years because you don't really feel anything else other than memory loss.

Music and Memory

Elderly people suffering from dementia were said to have better reasoning about their backgrounds and personal history when there was music playing in the clinical area than in silence, during an experiment conducted by Elizabeth Valentine, a psychologist at the University of London and co-author of new research on music and memory.

Increasingly, music is accompanying traditional medical therapies to help people heal faster. Experts say music has the power to calm and to energize the spirit.

The British researchers conducted a test on 23 people (ages 68 to 90) with mild dementia. The test was done with different sounds playing in the background.

While asking the questions, the researchers either played: a familiar tune (*Winter*, from Vivaldi's Four Seasons), novel music (*Hook*, by Fitkin), or pre-recorded cafeteria noise - or asked the questions in stillness. Over four weeks, each person was tested in all four situations.

The participants answered more questions correctly with sound in the background rather than in silence, and they scored even better when music was playing.

"Whether the music was familiar or new did not seem to matter. The music probably aroused the participants and helped them focus," the researchers said.

Sleep and Memory

Research indicates that you can better remember the information you are reading if you will go to sleep right after learning it. But there are two limits:

1. The material that you intend to recall should be easy to understand, or you should already have a fair amount of knowledge or experience in the topic being discussed.

2. You must not be too tired or exhausted when reading the material.

The next time you need to learn something, try this procedure and see if it works for you. It worked for me!

Learning and Emotions

As discussed earlier, emotions and feelings play a very important role in the process of learning and memory retention. Music has been said to affect learning and memory in psychologically-challenged patients. On the other hand, internal factors such as feelings and emotions should also be considered in retrieving data or in decoding stored information in your brain.

The creation of a good mood in producing better temper, positive outlooks, or even in relaxation are very popular nowadays in creating a holistic approach in wellness and mental health. The balance between mind and body and the conditioning that happens inside your brain may affect your acquisition of knowledge and information. That is why, it is very important to have a good mood in perceiving, receiving, and retrieving emotional as well as mental information.

Here are some of the valuable tips or techniques in mood conditioning that will definitely help you improve your mental capacities.

1. Close your eyes and repeat a chant that will help you recall a picture, a scenario or a very relevant experience. You

can also do this by repeating a very positive statement like: "No matter what you say or do to me, I'm still a worthwhile person!" Remembering such words can also boost confidence during exams or in periods of learning or even in daily struggles. By saying positive things regarding your life, you are increasing the chances of associating your experience with pleasant feeling, and this would help you remember more of the good things than the bad ones that could lead you down.

2. Imagine a face of someone who has put you down in some ways in the past (e.g. a family member, a teacher, a friend, or an ex lover). After getting the picture of his or her face, say, "No matter what you say or do to me, I'm still a worthwhile person!" This would relieve you and put you into a positive consciousness in dealing with people or strangers. Mental pictures can also relieve you from the stress brought about by bad or traumatic experiences.

3. There are physical ways of improving mood or the place where learning has to take place. Scented candles, aromatic objects, or the creation of illusion of relaxation (with the use of verdant or calmed colors such as pastel, earth tones, or non-solid shades) are some of the practical ways in helping you to relax while learning or acquiring knowledge or information. In uncontrolled environments which require

spontaneous reaction, it would still be best to create mental pictures (imagining the blueness and calmness of the sea, or the very refreshing scene of a green countryside) while undertaking learning tasks or actions.

Chapter Two

ATTENTION

Before you can expect to remember or memorize a thing, that thing must have been impressed clearly upon the records of your subconscious. And the main factor of the recording of impressions is that quality of the mind that we call **Attention**, which is the ability to focus and give meaning to a particular data or stimulus.

Our capability to process information is somewhat limited. Therefore, we must constantly select and decide which data are relevant and which are not. Stimuli or sensations that you perceive and organize into meaningful thoughts are selectively analyzed by your brain. If the stimuli or data is relevant or applicable for further use or access, your brain transfers this information to the long-term storage center. However, for this to happen, attention must take place

One of the most common causes of poor attention is the lack of interest. You are more inclined to remember the things in which you have been most interested, because in that emanation of interest there has been a high degree of attention exhibited. A person may have a very poor memory for many things; but when it comes to things in which his interest is involved, he often remembers the most intricate details. This is called involuntary attention. This type of attention does not require special effort or exertion because it follows upon interest, curiosity, or desire.

The other type of attention is called voluntary attention. This form of attention is granted upon objects not necessarily interesting, curious, or attractive. This requires the effort and usage of the will.

Every person has more or less involuntary attention, while only a few possess developed voluntary attention. The former is initiated by instinct, while the latter comes only by practice and training.

For attention to take place, you must diligently practice the art of voluntary attention. Here are some successful strategies to help you acquire this essential skill:

1. **Turn your attention upon some uninteresting thing and study every detail until you are able to describe them.**

This will seem boring or tiresome at first but you must stick to it. Do not practice too long at a time at first; take a rest and try it again later. You will soon find that it comes easier, and that a new interest is starting to manifest itself in the task. For example, pick a flower. Touch it. Smell it. Feel its texture. How many petals does it have? How long is the stem? What is the color and shape of the petals? By doing this simple task, you will be surprised at the quantity of little things that you will notice. This method, practiced on many things, in spare hours, will develop the power of voluntary attention and perception in anyone, no matter how deficient he or she may have been in these things. Begin to take notice of things about you: the places you visit, the people in the rooms, etc. In this way you will start the habit of "noticing things," which is the first requisite for memory development.

2. **Eliminate distractions.** Even though you may have heard of multi-tasking, it is very difficult for people to do more than one thing at a time. For example, you're a law student studying for the Bar Exams. You wouldn't be able to absorb properly into your mind what you are studying if your radio is playing loud rock-and-roll music, or if you're hearing the video games being played by your kid brother. As much as possible,

avoid any possible distractions such as TV, radio, or other people chattering.

3. **Retain focus and concentration in the process of learning or memorization.** Let's say you're busy preparing for an important presentation tomorrow. A new employee was introduced to you while you are working. In this case, there would be much less chance for you to remember anything about that new employee because you are concentrating on something else which you regard as more urgent or important. If you want to remember something well, shift your focus on that one thing and willfully commit it to memory.

4. **Keep track all of your thoughts.** Whenever you become aware that your thoughts are losing, yell "STOP!" in your mind. This will bring your drifting to a halt and redirect your attention to what needs to be done. Remember that good concentration breeds good memory. If you find that your thoughts are traveling, be conscious that your attention is drifting.

5. **Get interested.** To have good memorization skills, you should also like what you are doing. To vividly memorize a visual, an image, or even text, engage yourself into it. You should put your heart in every activity you're working and

doing. If you don't like to engage in a certain activity, there's a slim chance for you to remember aspects about it. Let's say your parents want you to become an engineer, but you dream of becoming a musician. If you studied engineering because your parents forced you to, you won't have the dedication or desire to retain information from your engineering books. Don't push yourself to do something that you have no interest in. As Leonardo Da Vinci said: *"Just as eating against one's will is injurious to health, so study without a liking for it spoils the memory, and it retains nothing it takes in."*

6. **Get motivated.** Now let's say you want to become a doctor. Why are you familiarizing and memorizing into such ambiguous medical or biological terms? For one thing, you might want to be on the top of the class. Or you might want to be popular in your school. Or you might want to be a good doctor someday to help your community. Goals and timeframe nourish motivation. And motivation promotes a sharp memory. To further motivate yourself, reward yourself for any tasks that you have accomplished. Set a particular incentive for every objective. For example, treat yourself to your favorite restaurant after finishing a project. When you've accomplished a bigger task, go on a vacation. Just set something gratifying to indulge

in after completing a certain undertaking. Remember: Man by nature is a go-getter. He will get whatever he aspires for. In a consumption-based and technologically-driven world, one should have a stake or goal to feed his symbolic ego. By rewarding yourself in every success you account for, you will aspire for more and will develop interest on your activity. In the process, your interest will make you more productive and successful.

7. **Give your subconscious a mental command to bear in mind what you want to remember.** You may say, "Here, you take note of this and remember it for me!" You'll be astounded by what the subconscious can do for you.

Before you can memorize or remember anything, you should be able to perceive well through proper attention. Use the methods above and you're well on your way to a sharper memory.

Chapter Three

BASIC MEMORY TOOLS

No one is born with a bad memory. Unless factors such as your lifestyle, health, or other conditions has affected it, you can sharpen your memory with the proper knowledge and practice. In this chapter, I'm going to discuss the basic concepts of memory.

Association

If you want to efficiently remember something, it is necessary that it be regarded in connection, or in association with one or more other things that you already know. The greater the number of other things with which it is associated with, the better chances you will be able to recall it.

Two popular techniques of association are acronyms and acrostics.

An acronym is an invented combination of first letters of the items to be remembered. For example: an acronym commonly used to remember the sequence of colors in the light spectrum is the name ROY G. BIV: Red, Orange, Yellow, Green, Blue, Indigo, and Violet. Sometimes, the acronym can be more familiar than the complete name itself, such as RAM (Random Access Memory) or SCUBA (Self-Contained Underwater Breathing Apparatus).

On the other hand, an acrostic is an invented sentence where the first letter of each word is a cue to the thing you want to remember. For example, **E**very **G**ood **B**oy **D**eserves **F**un is an acrostic to remember the order of G-clef notes on sheet music - E, G, B, D, F. An acrostic for the nine planets of our solar system would be **M**y **V**ery **E**ager **M**other **J**ust **S**ent **U**s **N**ine **P**eaches (Mercury, Venus, Earth, Mars, Jupiter, Saturn, Uranus, Neptune, Pluto).

Visualization and Imagination

Images are internal sensory representations that are also used in the creation of memory. They can bring words to mind, which can arouse other images or pictures. The formation of images appears to help in learning and remembering what has been learned or experienced in the past.

Images and words can help you in remembering things by bringing pictures in your head instead of just words or figures. Let's say, in learning the process of cell mitosis or cell division, most of the books that contain concepts or scientific ideas have pictures to describe scenarios that are sometimes difficult to be seen by the human eye. Another example would be the structure of a bacteria or a virus. Graphic elements and visual tools, therefore, may become guiding principles in learning conceptual or precisely scientific ideas.

Another example would be in memorizing the lyrics of the songs or in remembering stories that you might have read before. In these two examples, the memorization process becomes easier if you imagine the images conjured by the lyrics of the song or if you create vivid images in your mind as you read or recall a narrative or tale. Picture the actual scenario described by the sentences or paragraphs.

To further intensify your imagination, you have to actually feel what the character is feeling. If you're reading a story about a knight in shining armor fighting a dragon, then feel your strength, the power of your sword, the heat of the fire from the dragon's mouth, and even the kiss of the princess after saving her from the monster. ☺

Images and the formation of which, in the process of learning or remembering, can therefore help you in improving your memory. Here are some of the valuable methods which you can use in achieving an imaginative memory:

1. Learn to think with both words and figures. For example, in reading a book, it would be helpful to stop for a while and reconstruct the suggested scenario inside your head. This way, you are also increasing the chances of not only recording linguistic data but also some of the essential cognitive aspect of remembering, like the reconstruction of perceived or imagined senses in your brain. The smell and taste of ice cream, the redness of a strawberry, or the thickness or thinness of blood described in a crime novel that not only gives chill or excitement in reading but also makes your reading experience more memorable.

2. In learning new ideas, associate these concepts with a very particular image or picture that is very personal or relevant to you. Put some premium on what you already know or on what is easily conjured by your brain in experiencing these words (like in learning a new language or subject). Put some personal relationship with these words like knowing the origin of their

31

meanings (etymology) or by giving them a concrete symbol in your head.

3. If you're reading a very technical manual or theory pamphlet, what you can do is imagine yourself doing the scenario suggested by the book. This is also what we call as vivid reading. Words and sentences become alive not with their meaningful connections but with their correlative value with reality. In fact, writing prose or poetry involves a highly developed skill in imagery and mental mapping. Poets and creative writers are said to be good not only in remembering details or facts, but also in the creation of worlds or situations found within the mind.

Clustering

Grouping of details and data in recalling names or numbers is very essential in the process of retention. The associative power suggested by groups or grouped items help us further organize or give direction in memorization. Pairing words, for example, either synonymously or with their opposing meanings, like "fair" and "square" or "man" and "woman" helps us remember data more easily because they are not only singularly meaningful but at the same time relative to other words or data that we already know from the past.

Clustering numbers (memorizing telephone numbers by threes or by fours) or in whatever relevant grouping, is one tendency that leads to easy access from these numbers or even word groupings. Clustering is one way we can further improve our memory. Examples of these include:

1. Grouping by numbers, colors, or under the same category.

2. Grouping words and concepts by their opposing meanings or through antonyms: (bitter vs. sweet, love vs. hate)

3. Grouping words into pictures or through subjective organization.

Subjective organization depends on the way we recall or organize our materials by our own categories or devices. For example, learning a list of new words or vocabularies can be developed through subjective interpretations of these words or groupings. The better we organize or become aware of how we build a system of information, the better it would be in performing cognitive or mental tasks such as memorization or application of our memory.

One example of this is cooking. We may follow a recipe or procedure dictated by the recipe. But the way we cook food or give meaning to the process of cooking is different from one another. Thus, the procedure is also similar in getting information and knowledge. It would be better if you:

1. Think of the process of how you solve your problems or in getting the necessary information.

2. Know your capacity in the process of learning or memorization. Are you the type of person who easily gets the information by clustering them into meaningful categories, or are you the type of person who learns better if you follow a direction or picture inside your head?

3. Analyze the situation, the details, or experiences. Try to remember the relevant facts and remove unnecessary data or information.

Chapter Four

OVERCOMING FORGETFULNESS

"The existence of forgetting has never been proved: We only know that some things don't come to mind when we want them," Friedrich Nietzsche once said.

Being forgetful causes a lot of anxiety in people today, especially with the increasing awareness of memory-related diseases like Alzheimer's. On the other hand, new studies show that the human mind, not traumatized by serious injury or disease, never forgets. Experts say forgetting is not akin to losing information, but more so because there might be slip-up in the way the information was stored or in the way it is being retrieved.

But then, if the problem really lies on information-gathering and retrieval, why do most of us still tend to forget, no matter how hard we rack our brains? We forget where we put those keys, that much-needed item in the grocery list, or worse, those very important answers in an exam that might spell the difference between a passing mark and a failing grade.

A variety of factors contribute to the way our brain stores and supplies information. Although schools of thought and psychology are still debating on how the human mind works, they agree for one thing that memory is affected by our overall experience - from our genes, to the kind of childhood we had, down to the food we ate for breakfast this morning.

Some scientists liken the mind to a video camera because of its ability and nature to record everything a person experiences. Thus, looking for a particular event in your past is similar to searching for a scene in a video footage: a person can select the target scene, view it in slow motion or fast forward, even pause or zoom in to a particular detail. It is from this view that techniques to retrieve memory using hypnosis, truth serum, meditation, therapy and other similar forms come from.

On the other hand, despite the mind's "videographic" eye, it was discovered that the mind does not have perfect archival properties, similar to a videotape that can gather mildew, lose sharpness, and age over time. The brain is also likened to a computer chip. While it may hold very large amount of information, its capacity to store data nevertheless has its limitations. To make way for "new data," the mind reconstructs the stored information from time to time. Thus, events may not be perfectly remembered. Over time, some elements may be lost, details may get blurry or gradually be gone. "Trigger" elements such as a song, a photograph, or a kind of smell may bring back a long-forgotten memory. Still some fragments of our past can be gone forever.

In this chapter, we will discuss the ways and techniques on how humans, from scientists to mystics, deal with the trait of forgetting.

Forgetting is what we refer as the temporary or long-term loss of details, stimuli record, or memory materials that has been learned or stored in our brains. A forgotten item may be stored in memory but unavailable for retrieval or recall. There are several theories or explanation regarding forgetting.

1. **Decay of Memory Traces** - This is the oldest explanation regarding forgetting. Memory is said to have a natural tendency to decay with time. When a word or a name of person is no longer relevant, such memory item may eventually lose its significant place inside our brain.

2. **Distortion of Memory** - Some experiences may be learned or retrieved in a much distorted form. Such inaccuracy

may lead to a different or false memory or may even defeat the process of retrieval since what are being accessed are wrong traces or leads in our brain.

3. **Interference** - This experience may have been a result of in-between situations or uncontrollable variables during the experience of learning or memorizing. This also includes what occurs before, during, or after learning. Activities done before a task may confuse the retention process or what psychologists call as *proactive inhibition*. The more previously learned task there are, the greater the forgetting of the new tasks or operation. However, the more meaningful the material to be learned and retained, the less effect of such proactive kind of inhibition. On the other hand, an opposite effect happens during the *retroactive inhibition*, in which there are interfering activities occurring after a learning period. Usually, people who have to learn a second task forget more of the first than those who are given only one task to do. That is why, it would be advisable to master a particular task or skill before going on to the next activity, because retaining too much information require complex interactions of your memory and psychomotor skill. Such example is proven during the period of learning how to drive. Motor skills and various movements are necessary and may

sometimes look confusing at first since they require synchronicity. However as we slowly start to learn to put individual bodily tasks into a cohesive and unified action, we begin to think in a very precise and completely organized manner. This means we have already learned or memorized different tasks and have already put them into order. Therefore, in order to remember more, one must have mastery of a particular task or skill before engaging in other activities which require particular specialization.

4. **Motivated Forgetting** - This is a variable in forgetting which involve the individual's motive or desire to remember or forget. People seem to repress certain memories or suppress the process of retention or memory retrieval. More often remembered are pleasant events than unpleasant ones. Emotion also plays an important aspect in this explanation regarding forgetting. Some people prefer to forget experiences that are sad or traumatic. This may be a wise move. If you spend less time recollecting your failures and disappointments in life, you'll have better capacity to retain the positive and essential information in your mind. Because negative thoughts aggravate stress, you should learn to relax and forget about past mistakes. The past is done. Focus and retain only positive thoughts.

5. **Lack of Cues or Guides** - We are able to retrieve material to the extent that we have cues to remind us of it. When we remember something, it is as if we search our memory with the help of cues or guides that point the way to the desired materials. When we forget, it is because we may lack the necessary cues or guides in getting back the information stored in the vast neural connection of our brain.

Here are some effective techniques to overcome forgetfulness or absentmindedness:

1. **Write down your detailed list of "things to do."** Group or arrange your tasks into categories (and subcategories if applicable). Cross off activities that you have done and add new tasks along the way. If possible, stick your notes in objects that are familiar to you (television, refrigerator, entrance door, etc.)

2. **Use your imagination and humor.** Let's say you have an appointment with a potential client, Mr. Anderson, this coming Friday. If you love to watch TV every night, imagine Mr. Anderson acting like a clown on TV. You may even see him coming right out of the boob tube and saying, "See you on Friday!" To remember Friday better, you can visualize Mr. Anderson on your TV screen dressed as a chef and "frying" (Friday) some delicious foods. Come up with funny images that

will help you remember your schedule. The funnier and more exaggerated, the better.

3. **Associate a task with a routine activity or with something that you regularly do.** Let's say you always forget to bring your cell phone every time you go to work. See to it that before you brush your teeth or take a shower, you put your cell phone inside your bag. Just make a task that you often forget a part of your daily routine.

4. **Create a visual hint.** Let's say you invited your boss to dinner at your house on Tuesday night, and you must buy some potatoes for the dessert you'll be cooking. With your very busy schedule, you can easily forget to buy it. To aid you in remembering, you may put a pack of potato chips or a toy potato at the top of your TV or in the middle of your dining table to remind you of the task that needs to be done.

5. **Focus and say your task out loud.** Have you ever experienced coming up to your friend because you want to ask something? Next thing you know, you completely forgot the things you're going to inquire him. Well, don't panic. Many people have been in your situation and you're not alone. With today's hectic lifestyle, even those with good memory can forget what they're thinking about in a split second. The solution here

is to focus on one task at a time, and repeatedly say out loud what you're going to do: "I'm going to ask John about the rules in joining his contest." If in case you still forget about what you're going to do, try going back to your place of origin where you said the task out loud. Oftentimes, that specific place would help you to recall your task by associating that location with what you have said.

6. **Don't procrastinate.** If you have a certain activity that needs to be done, get it over with as early as you can. When you need to pay your bills, do it now before it becomes overdue and before it starts charging interest. If you really can't attend to it now, then use your imagination, visual reminders, or other helpful tools to remember it.

7. **Get a companion.** Some people living in solidarity can become absentminded and can suffer memory loss. That's because they don't have anyone to talk to, so their mental capacity is limited and not utilized well. Having a smart companion to discuss various topics with, and to share your knowledge and experiences with, can sharpen you memory. They can even act as your back-up. Just tell them to remember something and you'll have another memory working on your behalf. Just be nice to your buddy.

Chapter Five

MEMORY AND YOUR SENSES

Did you know that the impressions received from your five senses of sight, hearing, taste, touch, and smell have a significant role in the retention of information in your mind? These are called Memory of Sense Impressions. However, when you come down to a systematic analysis of sense impressions retained in the memory, you'll find that the majority of such impressions are those acquired through the two respective senses: sight and hearing.

Sight Impressions

We are constantly exercising our sense of sight, and receiving thousands of different sight impressions every hour. But most of these impressions are insignificantly recorded upon the memory, because we give them little attention or interest.

Before the memory can be stored with sight impressions, before the mind can recollect or remember such impressions, the eye must be used under the direction of the attention. We think that we see things when we look at them, but in reality we see only a few aspects, in the sense of registering clear and unique impressions of them upon the depths of the subconscious mind. We look at them as a whole rather than see them in detail.

For example, there was a man who was attacked by a robber. The man had a close view of the thief's face. When the victim went to the nearby police station to report the unfortunate incident, he was asked by the police officer to describe the criminal in details. The victim, although having a close view of the man's face, was unable to give an accurate description to the police. He was unable to perceive well because he's in a state of nervousness and shock while the thief was assaulting him.

This is a case of "looking without seeing." The way to train the mind to receive clear sight-impressions, and therefore to retain them in the memory, is simply to concentrate the will and attention upon objects of sight, endeavoring to see them plainly and distinctly, and then to practice recalling the details of the object some time afterward.

Will and attention would not be effective if not combined with interest. You must have the desire or passion to really accomplish the task at hand. Shift your mental focus, by means of will and attention coupled with interest, to overcome the mere "seeing and observing" phenomena. In order to remember the things that pass before your sight, you must begin to see with your mind, instead of just looking with your eyes. Let the impression get beyond your retina and into your mind. If you will do this, you will find that memory will "do it's thing."

Hearing Impressions

Many sounds reach the ear but are not retained by the mind. We may pass along a noisy street, the waves of many sounds reaching the nerves of the ear, and yet the mind accepts the sounds of only a few things, particularly when the novelty of the sounds has passed away. It is again a matter of interest and attention in this case.

To acquire the faculty of correct hearing, and correct memory of things heard, the mental faculty of hearing must be exercised, trained and developed. It is a fact that the mind will hear the faintest sounds from things in which is centered interest and attention, while at the same time ignoring things in which there is no interest and to which the attention is not turned. A sleeping mother will wake up at the slightest cry from her baby, while the booming sound of drums in a parade, or even the firing of a gun in the vicinity may not be noticed by her. A skilled physician will detect the faint sounds indicating a respiratory or cardiovascular illness in patients. However, these same people who are able to detect the faint differences in sound, above mentioned, are often known as "poor hearers." The reason is because they hear only that in which they are interested, and to which their attention has been diverted. That is the whole secret, and in it is also to be found the secret of training of the ear-perception. The remedy for "poor hearing," and poor memory of things heard depends on your level of interest and attention.

The reason that many persons do not remember things that they have heard is simply because they have not listened properly. One cannot listen to everything, as it would not be advisable. Persons who have poor memories of ear-impressions should begin to "listen" attentively. You will find the following technique helpful:

Try to remember words, phrases, or sentences that are spoken to you in a conversation. You will find that the effort made to imprint the sentence on your memory will result in a concentration of the attention on the words of the speaker. Do the same thing when you are listening to a teacher, singer, actor,

46

or lecturer. Pick out the words for memorizing, and make up your mind that your memory will receive the impression easily and retain it well. Listen to the tiny bits of dialogue that come to your ears while walking on the street, and aim to memorize a sentence or two, as if you're going to relate them to another person. Study the expressions and inflections in the voices of persons speaking to you. You will be astonished at the details that such examination will reveal.

. Listen to the tones of various people and strive to distinguish the differences in sound between them. Have your friend read a line or two of poetry, and then endeavor to memorize it. Keep doing this and you will significantly develop the power of voluntary attention to sounds and spoken words. But above everything else, practice repeating the words and sounds that you have memorized, as many times as possible. By doing this, you will get the mind into the habit of taking an interest in sound impressions.

2-in-1 Combo

In some cases the impressions of sight and sound are joined together, as for instance in the case of words, in which not only the sound but the shape of the letters composing the word, or rather the word-shape itself, are stored away together, and consequently are far more readily recalled or remembered than things of which only one sense impression is recorded.

Teachers of memory use this information as a means of helping their students to remember words by speaking them aloud, and then writing them down. Many persons memorize names in this way, the impression of the written word being added to the impression of the sound, thus doubling the potential.

The more impressions that you can make regarding a thing, the greater the chances of easily remembering it. Likewise it is very important to attach an impression of a weaker sense, to that of a stronger one, in order that the former may be memorized. For instance, if you have a good eye memory, but a poor ear memory, it is suggested to connect your sound impressions to the sight impressions. And if you have a poor eye memory but a good ear memory, it is important to link your sight impressions to your sound impressions. In this way, you take advantage of the law of association.

Chapter Six

HOW TO REMEMBER NAMES AND FACES

You have probably heard a similar statement that says, "The most beautiful word an individual can ever hear is his or her own name being called by another person."

However, this poses a great threat to people who have trouble remembering names, especially those who are frequently attending important business meetings and gatherings. If someone approaches you and called you by your first name, wouldn't it be embarrassing if you don't reciprocate by saying his or her name back? And of course, it's more humiliating to directly ask his or her name when that person expects you to know it.

The same thing stands true for remembering faces. Wouldn't it bother you to have met successful entrepreneurs in a gathering, only to forget how they look like when you get home?

More often than not, the difficulty in remembering names and faces is caused by the fact that names and faces in themselves are uninteresting, and therefore do not pull in or hold attention as do other objects presented to the mind.

Here are effective strategies to help you remember names and faces easily:

1. **Instead of merely listening to the faint sound of a name, focus on hearing it clearly and concentrate on firmly implanting it on your memory**.

2. **Repeatedly say the name many times over in your mind.** If possible, use the name as often as possible. You can tell your friend now, and then your sister later: "I've just met Jonathan Nowitzki." You can also make a comment about his name: "I have a former classmate named Mark Nowitzki who is very good in electronics. Do you know him?"

3. **After hearing the name, write it down several times.** By doing this, you are acquiring the benefit of a double sense impression, adding eye impression to ear impression.

4. When you hear the name of a person being spoken, look purposefully at the person bearing it. By doing this, you are connecting the name and the face together in your mind at the same time. The next time you forget the name, just recall the face and you might have a good chance of remembering it.

5. Visualize the name as an object in your mind. See the name's letters in your mind's eye, as an image or picture. Exaggerate it as much as you can. You can imagine the name "Nowitzki" in your mind as a big hairy object with 3 eyes and with spikes all over it. For a clearer image, visualize Mr. Nowitzki himself lifting the giant word "Nowitzi" over his head, like a weightlifter lifting a barbell. The more exaggerated or humorous, the better chances it will get stuck in your mind.

6. Connect a new person with a well-remembered individual of the same name. Associate a new Mr. Coppenhagen with an old customer of the same name. When you see the new man, you would think of the old one, and the name would flash into your mind. You can even visualize the 2 Coppenhagens attached to each other like Siamese Twins, to trigger the thought that they have the same name.

7. **Reminisce the atmosphere or environment.** Recalling what you felt or what you did, when you met a person, could trigger memories of how he or she was introduced to you, how he or she looked like, and other aspects regarding the person.

8. **Analyze the distinctive features of the person's face.** Notice what makes that individual stand out or different from the rest. You may notice the eyes, nose, ears, lips, hair, or other parts of the face. Such notice and recognition tend to induce an interest in the subject of features. It forces you to focus on the person's face the first time you meet him or her. Right now, you know the importance of having interest to remember things. If you were introduced to a man who would pay you over $500 on your next meeting, you would be very inclined to memorize his name and to study his face carefully to recognize him, as opposed to a man who has nothing to give to you.

9. **Link a name with a visual object.** Let's say you just met Mr. Quinlan. To remember his name, you can visualize a land full of queens (Quinlan). Imagine the queens dressed in elegant dresses and wearing shiny crowns with big jewels. If Mr. Quinlan is interested in basketball and you want to remember that too, then imagine the queens wearing basketball

uniforms over their elegant dresses, and shooting hoops. And if Mr. Quinlan is also a doctor, then visualize the queens in basket ball uniforms, having large stethoscopes around their necks, shooting hoops. You can even imagine the queens saying in a bugs bunny-like way, "Nyieh. What's up doc?" The funnier, the better. Here's another example, but this time with a longer name. Let's say you've been introduced to Mary Bennetton. Now how do you remember "Bennetton?" You can divide it into "Bend-a-ton." Imagine a large piece of metal with the words "1 ton" engraved at all its sides bending like a soft pillow. You can exaggerate it a little bit by making that piece of metal cry in agony as the bending is taking place. If Ms. Bennetton is a tennis player, you can imagine the bending piece of metal having tennis rackets stuck on top of its head.

10. **Visualize the faces of persons you have met during the day, in the evening.** Try to develop the faculty of visualizing their features to practice your ability. Draw them in your mind and see them with your mind's eye, until you can visualize the features of very old friends. Then do the same with acquaintances, and so on, until you are able to visualize the features of every one you know. Then start to add to your list by recalling the features of strangers whom you meet. By a little

practice of this kind you will develop a great interest in faces and your memory of them, and the power to recall them will increase rapidly.

11. **Make a study of names and faces.** Start a collection, and you will have no trouble in developing a memory for them. A good idea would be to analyze photographs in detail, not as a whole. If you can incite adequate interest in names and faces, you will be more prone to remember them.

Chapter Seven

HOW TO REMEMBER NUMBERS

In almost everything we do, there are numbers involved - telephone numbers, credit card and ATM numbers, zip codes, passwords, calculations, and many others! Whether you love them or you hate them, numbers are here to stay. In order to cope up with today's hectic lifestyle, you have to be able to remember a lot of numbers, or you'll end up getting all confused and disorganized.

Contrary to words that can be associated with an object, numbers are difficult to remember because they are abstract. If I say think of a pen, your mind immediately visualizes the pen. But if I say 2473, you will have a hard time committing it to memory.

In this chapter, you'll be taught various memory techniques to remember numbers better so you can perform your usual transactions quicker and more efficiently.

Senses

Your senses, particularly the ears and eyes, may prove to be effective in recalling numbers. Here's how it works:

Repeat the number several times to yourself. It may be difficult for you to remember a number such as "2895" as an abstract thing, but easy for you to remember the sound of "twenty-eight ninety-five."

You may also visualize the number. Write it down several times to lodge it to your memory bank. An even better idea is to create a vivid image of that number for better memory retention. Visualize "2895" beautifully laid out on a billboard in large sizes and luminous colors, with pieces of jewelry all around it. The number just follows you wherever you go. You see it everywhere. It's on your bathroom mirror, on the TV screen, in the fireplace, it just won't let you go! You can even intensify the image by making a jingle or slogan like "2895, I like you to jive!"

You may forget that the number of a certain house or office is 2895, but you may easily remember the sound of the spoken words "two-eight-nine-five," or the form of "2895" as you see it on the door of the place.

Association

The Law of Association may be used advantageously in memorizing numbers. For instance, one might remember the number 186,000 (the number of miles per second traveled by light-waves in the ether) by associating it with the number of his father's former place of business, "186." Another person may remember his zip code "1876" by recalling the date of the Declaration of Independence.

Converting Numbers to Words

One very common yet practical technique to remember numbers is to transform them to words. Probably the easiest way to do this is to assign each number 1 to 9 a letter equivalent: A=1, B=2, C=3, D=4, and so on. Using this technique, 742 turns into GDB. The letters GDB doesn't make much sense, so you have to turn it into an acrostic. How about "Great Dancing Bellies?" The next time you want to recall 742, just recall

"Great Dancing Bellies" and convert the first letters of each word back to their number equivalents. If you think the phrase "Great Dancing Bellies" may still slip your mind, create an image of fat tummies dancing merrily to the beat of the drum.

Here's another example. If you need to remember your system password which is 135, then you may imagine your computer "Allowing Cute Entrance" to someone as adorable as you.

The Picture Code

Using this technique, you assign an image to each number 1 to 9 that is similar to its appearance. See how the numbers below look like the objects they are representing:

0 = ball

1 = magic wand

2 = swan

3 = fork

4 = sailboat

5 = seahorse

6 = bomb

7 = crowbar

8 = hourglass

9 = balloon

Memorize all the symbols above and their number equivalents. If you find that these symbols do not stick in your mind, then convert them to something that you can remember better. After memorizing the images, you can begin using this method.

Let's say you want to remember the street number of your friend's home, which is 289. You can then visualize a swan (2) swimming with an hourglass (8) at it's back; and tied to the hourglass is a big red balloon (9). Or let's say you want to remember 471. You can imagine a sailboat (4) with a crowbar (7) hanging at its side; and glued to the crowbar is a long wand (1).

The Major Memory System

This method is a bit complicated and detailed; but once you get the hang of it, you can remember long strings of numbers and you can even impress your friends! In this method, each number is assigned a consonant or a consonant sound based on the following:

0 = s, z, soft-c ("z" is first letter of zero)

1 = t ("t" is similar to a 1 with a line through it)

2 = n ("n" has two bars)

3 = m ("m" has three bars)

4 = r ("r" is last letter of four)

5 = L ("L" is Roman numeral for 50)

6 = j, sh, ch, soft-g ("g" is 6 rotated 180 degrees)

7 = k ("k" looks like two 7s rotated and pasted together)

8 = f, v ("f" written in cursive has two loops similar to 8)

9 = p, b ("p" and "b" looks like 9 in different angles)

Here's how this system works. Get the consonant or consonant sounds of the numbers, and add vowels between them to form a group of words, phrase, or sentence.

Let's say the phone number you want to remember is 854-0341. Convert that to "flr-smrt." Add some vowels and you will come up with something like "flower smart." The next time you need to access that phone number, just remember "flower smart." You can even add a dash of visualization and humor by imagining a flower with thick glasses and a diploma, reading "Theory of Relativity."

List of Memory Words

Let's take the Major Memory System to the next level. (Refer to the table in the previous lesson) What you're going to do with the consonants or consonant sounds is to make a list of words that relate to them. Let me give you some samples below:

1 = t = toe

2 = n = Noah

3 = m = Ma

4 = r = rat

5 = L = Law

6 = j = jaw

7 = k = key

8 = f = fee

9 = p = pea

0 = z = zoo

What about numbers with double digits? The word must start with the consonant representing the first number, and must end with the consonant representing the second digit. Examples are below:

10 = ts = toes

11 = tt = teeth

12 = tn = tin

13 = tm = Tom

14 = tr = tire

15 = tL = tail

16 = tg = tag

17 = tk = tack

18 = tf = Tif

19 = tb = tub

20 = ns = nose

These list of memory words will help you associate something with a number. For example, you made a list of things to do at your house and task number 7 is cleaning the refrigerator. Connect the key (assigned image of 7) with the appliance. You can visualize a large key stuck in your refrigerator door. If task number 9 is cleaning the toilet, you can imagine lots of peas (assigned image of 9) floating in the toilet bowl.

This advanced tool can be pretty helpful in remembering items that are arranged in chronological order. For example, in the Ten Commandments, you want to know Commandment Number 4 (Respect thy father and thy mother). So you visualize your parents in elegant clothes holding white rats in their hands.

Once you've become familiar with the words you've made up to represent the numbers, you'll be able to recall any item on a list just by hearing its number, regardless of the arrangement.

But how many words should you create? That depends on your necessity. Many people have a list of a hundred words. Although that may seem extensive, as long as you know the consonant or consonant sounds representing each number, you have nothing to worry about.

Remembering Dates

The Major Memory System, combined with a witty visualization, can also be used to remember special dates.

Let's say you need to remember your friend's birthday, which is May 11. You can visualize your friend with a birthday hat asking *"May* I clean your teeth?" ("Teeth" represents the number 11, see table above).

How about if you want to remember a party scheduled on Sunday at 4:00 p.m.? For days of the week, you may assign a number for each. (e.g. Sunday = 1, Monday = 2, Tuesday = 3, and so on).

Now we do the translation: 14 (1 being Sunday and 4 being 4:00 p.m.) For 14, we've assigned the image of tire. A visualization of a wild party with tires being thrown everywhere would be a great reminder that you have a party on Sunday at 4:00 p.m.

What if it's 4:30? Or 4:15? Well, simply use the words quarter, half, and three quarters to represent the different parts of an hour (15 minutes past, 30 minutes past, and 45 minutes past). Then you can inject it into your visualization.

For the example above, you can include quarters being showered (aside from the tires) if the party starts at 4:15.

What if it's 4:25? Choose the nearest quarter hour so you won't be late!

Remembering Channels

You can sometimes end up confused over the many TV channels that we have nowadays; therefore, you may forget some or a lot of them. Here's how to solve this dilemma:

Let's take NBC (National Broadcasting Company, Channel 7) for example. You can turn the letters NBC into an acrostic like **N**aughty **B**ig **C**ats. Visualize the largest unusual cats you've ever seen, with bright green eyes and the longest tails possible, running wildly all over the place. To remember 7, convert it into its word equivalent which is "key." So to remember that NBC is channel 7, imagine **N**aughty **B**ig **C**ats playing around with large, shiny keys.

Chapter Eight

HOW TO REMEMBER PLACES

Different people have different abilities. Some are bestowed with the gift of direction. They are the ones who never forget how to arrive at a place of destination, no matter if they have to go through a labyrinth-like path to get there, and even though they've only been to that place once.

However, there are many people who do not possess that keen sense of direction. These are the people who just can't seem to remember the places they've went to, even if they've been to these locations several times before. Well, there's no need to get frustrated.

The first concept necessary to develop a good sense of direction is to have a deep interest in the places. You should begin to "take notice" of the direction of the streets or roads over which you travel - the landmarks; the turns of the road, even the natural objects along the way. Studying maps could help in awakening a new interest in them.

One of the first things to do, after arousing an interest, is to carefully note the landmarks and relative positions of the streets or roads over which you travel. So many people travel along a new street or road in an absent-minded manner, ignoring the features of the land as they proceed. This is fatal to place-memory. You must take notice of the thoroughfares and the things along the way. Pause at the cross roads, or the street-corners and note the landmarks, and the general directions and relative positions, until they are firmly retained on your mind. When you go jogging or walking, start to see how many things you can remember. And when you return home, go over the trip in your mind, and see how much of the direction and how many of the landmarks you are able to remember. Take out your pencil, and attempt to make a map of your itinerary, giving the general directions, and noting the street names, and distinct features of objects along the way.

Then as you travel along, compare places with your map, and you will find that you will take an entirely new interest in the trip. You will see that you can now notice things you were not able to recognize before.

Remembering Directions

It may be difficult to remember directions because of too many bits of repetitious, unfamiliar data being fed into your mind. If you're going to remember a lot of left and right turns amidst all the roads and blocks you'll be traveling, chances are, you will get totally confused.

What you have to do is to ask for a landmark. If your friend tells you to "turn right after the third block," you can ask what landmark you will see when you turn right. If your buddy answers that it's a barber shop, then you will certainly know in what block you will turn right to.

Another dilemma would be on how to remember all the "lefts" and "rights." The solution is simple. You can convert "left" and "right" into clear images that represent these words. For example, you can use "lizards" for left and "rats" for right. So if your friend tells you to "turn right after the third block," you can imagine large furry rats scurrying all over the barber shop. If you can exaggerate it further, like visualizing the rats in sunglasses and gangster clothes, you can remember it even better.

Remembering Addresses

You can also use the methods you've previously learned in remembering addresses. For example, you want to remember 32 Cottonwood Avenue. You can turn 32 into moon (3 = m, 2 = n, then add vowels). Then for Cottonwood, you can visualize a large plank of dancing wood with cotton all over its body, eating cotton candy. Then link everything together. How about that large plank of wood with cotton all over its body, sharing and feeding some cotton candy to the bright round moon. Can you see them bond together so closely that they look like a perfect couple?

For larger numbers like 142, you can convert that to train (1 = t, 4 = r,

2 = n). You can visualize that cotton-covered wood riding a very happy train while they're singing a lively song together.

See? Not only do these methods help you to remember, but they are fun to do. Just keep on practicing. And don't think this is a chore. Have fun imagining things and you'll end up with a far better memory than ever before.

Chapter Nine

HOW TO REMEMBER EVENTS

Can you still remember what your breakfast was 3 days ago? Can you recall what your boss announced yesterday regarding the company's new mission statement?

Don't panic if things like these escape your memory. You're not alone. Sometimes, we become too engrossed with a lot of our daily responsibilities that we tend to forget events or happenings we haven't paid much attention to.

If you will give to the occurrences of each day a mental review in the evening, you will find that the act of reviewing will engage the attention to register the events in such a manner that they will be available anytime for future retrieval.

Let this work be done in the evening, when you feel at ease. Do not do it after you retire. The bed is made for sleep, not for thinking. You will find that the subconscious will awaken to the fact that it will be called upon later for the records of the day, and will "take notice" of what happens, in a far more diligent and faithful manner.

Try this exercise. Sit down alone one night and spend fifteen minutes attempting silently to remember exactly the important happenings of the day. You may find that you could recall only little at first. You may not even recall what you had for breakfast. But after a few days of practice, you will find that you could recall more. Events will come back to you more precisely and more clearly than at first. If possible, relate to people close to you, the events of the day instead of recalling them to yourself. If the people you're relating the events to are interested in them too, you would become more motivated to remember them.

Chapter 10

OTHER MEMORY TOOLS

Just when you thought you already know a lot of memory tools and techniques, we have more in store for you in this chapter.

Memory Organization

Being disorganized can surely take up a lot of your time, and it can negatively affect your efficiency. Your memory works the same way. Much like folders in a filing cabinet, you can also create mental folders to retain details in an organized manner.

How do we do this?

We create mental folders out of aspects that we can never forget or that are stored in our long-term memory, like days of the week and parts of the body. For this example, we shall take the parts of the body which are the hair, eyes, nose, lips, shoulders, chest, tummy, thighs, knees, and foot. Please take note that you can choose other body parts that are more familiar to you.

Let's say you have a list of tasks to do. If task number 1 is watering the plants, you can imagine your hair having flowers and leaves growing all over it. The flowers in your hair are happily dancing about as they are enjoying the fresh feeling of water being showered upon them. If task number 2 is cooking fried chicken for dinner, you can visualize your eyeballs to be shaped like whole chicken. The chicken looks so juicy while being fried to perfection.

Do this with the rest of your tasks. Assign a task to each file folder and create an exaggerated and humorous visualization for it. Have fun.

The Story Method

This method requires the creation of a whole story, but it doesn't have to be extensive as long as all the things to remember are included in the story. It establishes a connection between all the objects, where the sequence of events are easier to remember.

For example, your best friend requested you to serve these 7 dishes on his extravagant homecoming party, namely: prawn, crab, spinach, salmon, roast beef, pasta, and pizza. To remember them, you can come up with a similar story like this: The prawn and crab were walking side by side until the spinach came and yelled at them to pay their debts. Salmon and roast beef came along to stop the quarrel, but pasta and pizza showered them all with a water hose because of the disrupting noise being created.

It doesn't matter if your story sounds silly. You're not writing a book or report anyway. And remember, the sillier the story, the easier it is to remember.

The Facts Association

We are continually acquiring items of information regarding all kinds of subjects, and yet when we wish to collect them, we often find the task rather difficult, even though the original impressions were quite clear. This is because we have not properly classified and indexed our bits of information, and do not know where to begin to search for them. It is like the confusion of the entrepreneur who kept all of his papers in a cabinet, without index, or order. He knew that "they are all there," but he had hard work to find any one of them when it was required.

When you wish to consider a fact, ask yourself the following questions about it:

1. Where did it come from or originate?

2. What caused it?

3. What history or record has it?

4. What are its attributes, qualities and characteristics?

5. What things can I most readily associate with it? What is it like!

6. What is it good for - how may it be used - what can I do with it?

7. What does it prove - what can be deduced from it?

8. What are its natural results - what happens because of it?

9. What is its future; and its natural or probable end or finish?

10. What do I think of it, on the whole - what are my general impressions regarding it?

11. What do I know about it, in the way of general information?

12. What have I heard about it, and from whom, and when?

If you will take the trouble to put any "fact" through the above rigid examination, you will not only attach it to hundreds of convenient and familiar other facts, so that you will remember it readily upon occasion, but you will also create a new subject of general information in your mind of which this particular fact will be the central thought.

The more other facts that you manage to associate with any one fact, the more pegs you will have to pull that fact into the field of consciousness and the more cross indexes will you have whereby you may "run down" the fact when you need it.

7 Principles of Memory

The principles below may be applied to every aspect of your daily life: at home, at school, at work, and in your leisure time. Know that memory definitely involves learning, and both are complimentary activities for better survival and achievement in our modern world.

1. Learners learn from their behavior. Thus, learner errors should be minimized in order to achieve better memory and mastery of skills.

2. Learning is most effective when correct responses are reinforced immediately. Feedback should be informative and

rewarding whenever the response is correct as discussed above regarding memory and motivation. Punishment may be effective if used but data also shows that it may also inhibit learning than increase learning and memory improvement. It may temporarily suppress an incorrect response, but the response tends to reappear when the punishment stops. Punishment can also be emotionally disruptive and may become an interfering cognitive dissonance in the process of learning and storing of information. For example, children who are punished for making an error while reading aloud may become so upset and distracted by the punishment that they will commit more mistakes.

3. The frequency of reinforcement determines how well a response will be learned and retained.

4. Practicing a response in a variety of setting increases both retention of data and the transferability of these data into other information. This means one may involve a constant rethinking of ideas or imaging the self in a reactive activity (silently talking to oneself in order to elicit conscious response) in order to enhance better thinking and memory.

5. Motivated conditions may influence the effectiveness of positive thinking and memory and may play a key role in increasing the level of performance in memory retention.

6. Meaningful learning is more permanent and more transferable than memorized learning. Understanding what is memorized is better than just practicing how to become a good memorizer.

7. People learn more effectively when they learn at their own pace.

CONCLUSION

At this point, you've learned a bunch of techniques for memorizing things more effectively: forming vivid and funny images, making associations, converting numbers to picture words, and many others.

Remember, there is no "right" or "wrong" way to memorize something; the idea is to simply take the information and techniques you've already learned and adapt them to the specific task or activity at hand.

But above everything else, I encourage you to practice memorizing things every day. Consider this: If someone teaches you how to drive an automobile, and you study the car owner's manual carefully, and learn perfectly everything there is to know about driving a car, that doesn't mean you can jump in a car and start driving flawlessly in downtown New York City! You know what you need to do. Keep on practicing the memory techniques you've learned until they become second nature. Look around you and find things to memorize, such as your cousin's telephone number, your favorite chocolate chip cookie recipe, the call letters of your local TV stations, the vocabulary words in your school science textbook, your license plate or driver's license, or whatever! Go for it, and remember to have lots of fun!

9 784381 677006

Printed by Libri Plureos GmbH in Hamburg, Germany